"Read, believe, and just do it! I have worked with many consultants in my career but never has anyone showed me how to increase my production and reduce my stress like Sean Crabtree. My production was at its highest, stress level at its lowest and my team made more money than they ever had with me. We worked together until I sold my practice. My only regret was that I didn't find him earlier in my career."

Mitch Conditt, DDS
Diplomate ABCDSM, Fellow AACP

"Sean Crabtree's book is a critical read if you want to reduce stress and increase the profitability of your practice. While working with Sean and implementing the methodology in this book, my practice was not only transformed financially, it also made it much more enjoyable for me personally!"

Frank M. Walerko, DDS

"In working with Sean Crabtree for nearly a decade, I can tell you it's like having a personal trainer for your dental practice. He has kept the entire team focused on their vision and goals to make the practice a win-win for everyone, including the patients. His business background and experience working with so many dental offices gives him insight to the struggles that many offices contend with daily. The guidelines that Sean provides in this book can organize and assure all types of businesses continual growth and stability in this ever-changing market. This is a must read."

Stephen D. Poss, DDS
Diplomate, ABCDSM, ACSDD;
Fellow, AACP

"I've been working with dentists and their teams for over forty years and have observed many approaches to practice efficiency and team management. If a practice is feeling stuck, or a dentist feels it'd be impossible to work any harder in the practice, then they need to read Sean's message. His approach will not only boost a practice's profitability and team cohesion but also help it deliver a higher level of patient care and satisfaction. I've seen Sean transform the lives of our clients. It's all about the mindset!"

Don Brunker, CEO
Goetze Dental
Kansas City, MO

"Being mentored by Sean Crabtree has above all things allowed me to achieve a complete culture shift in my dental practice and in my personal life! I no longer believe in limits. Anything can be accomplished once you get limiting beliefs out of the way and replace them with ones that support your goals and vision. I no longer believe in just employees. My new standard is a reciprocating partnership with each and every team member. Instead of taking away from my personal life which I strongly believe happens to most owners, my dental business is the vehicle that allows me to achieve my personal goals. I cannot thank Sean enough for this long lasting relationship!"

Alvin Daboul DDS

DENTAL PROFITS

HOW TO MULTIPLY YOUR DENTAL PRACTICE REVENUE WITHOUT MULTIPLYING THE NUMBER OF NEW PATIENTS

SEAN CRABTREE

Dental Profits: How to Multiply Your Dental Practice Revenue without Multiplying the Number of New Patients Copyright © 2020 by Sean Crabtree.

All rights reserved. No part of this publication may be reproduced, distributed, or transmitted in any form or by any means, including photocopying, recording, or other electronic or mechanical methods, without the prior written permission of the author, except in the case of brief quotations embodied in critical reviews and certain other noncommercial uses permitted by copyright law.

Disclaimer:

The author strives to be as accurate and complete as possible in the creation of this book, notwithstanding the fact that the author does not warrant or represent at any time that the contents within are accurate due to the rapidly changing nature of the Internet.

While all attempts have been made to verify information provided in this publication, the Author and the Publisher assume no responsibility and are not liable for errors, omissions, or contrary interpretation of the subject matter herein. The Author and Publisher hereby disclaim any liability, loss or damage incurred as a result of the application and utilization, whether directly or indirectly, of any information, suggestion, advice, or procedure in this book. Any perceived slights of specific persons, peoples, or organizations are unintentional.

In practical advice books, like anything else in life, there are no guarantees of income made. Readers are cautioned to rely on their own judgment about their individual circumstances to act accordingly. Readers are responsible for their own actions, choices, and results. This book is not intended for use as a source of legal, business, accounting or financial advice. All readers are advised to seek the services of competent professionals in legal, business, accounting, and finance field.

Printed in the United States of America

ISBN: 978-1-948382-07-6 paperback
JMP2020.6

To Jenny and Marilee – my reasons for all things.

Contents

Introduction 1
Chapter 1: Challenge Your Own Thinking 7
    Be, Do, Have 8
    Identify Your References 12
    Shift Your Mindset 16

Chapter 2: Learn (and Believe) Why People Buy 19
    Why Do People Buy? 20
    It's Not about Price, It's about Value 23
    It's Not about Logic, It's about Emotion . 28

Chapter 3: Getting Clear on How to Create Value 31
    ENLIST 37
    Engage the Patient 38

 Inquiring and Listening............................ 43

 Intensification.. 44

 The Handover.. 46

 The After Diagnosis Wrap-Up 48

Chapter 4: Everyone Gets Involved 51

 The Intake Call 52

 The Customer Service ENLIST.................. 63

 The Financial Arrangement 66

Chapter 5: Define the Roles, Focus on Outcomes, and Excite Your Team........................... 75

 Clearly Defining Roles 76

 Think about Outcomes with Your Team.... 80

 Team Bonuses 83

Chapter 6: What to Track, When to Track, and How to Use the Information 87

 Commitment to Tracking........................... 87

 Accepted Is Paid For 89

 How to Have Meetings.............................. 93

CHAPTER 7: COACH IT CONSISTENTLY AND REAP THE REWARDS 98

    GIVING IT TO YOU STRAIGHT 100

    WTF 103

    TOUGH-NO 104

REFERENCES 107

Introduction

It was the end of October and as I arrived at my home airport in Nashville, exhausted, I began calculating how many hours I had until my flight the next day to San Diego. While driving home, my wife suggested that I get away for a little while, go visit our family farm, maybe do some hunting or, if nothing else, just watch the sunset. Looking back, I can tell you it was a destiny moment.

That trip turned into a 12-gauge shot to the head—literally to my head—from about forty yards away. I was airlifted to Vanderbilt University Medical Center, and immediately rushed to surgery. After surgery and a horrible night in the trauma center, the surgeon told me that one pellet was a millimeter from my carotid artery.

What followed was a year with paralyzed vocal cords, retina surgery, and much, much reflection. I was killing myself. With clients in five time zones and a travel schedule that amounted to nearly 205 days a year away from my family, something had to change. The realization hit me that time is my most valuable asset and that I had to become much more intentional about how I allowed it to be spent.

In the years leading up to this point, I would travel anywhere, anytime, for anyone who asked for my help. The clients who were implementing my strategies, many of them in this book, were massively successful. The ones who weren't, were not successful, and worse, they were draining the life from me and robbing me of my most valuable asset: time.

My goal was to positively impact the lives of my clients and my family, as well as my own life, and yet now the realization hit me that I had not kept this foremost in my mind—I had simply been working and working hard. I could no longer allow my time to be spent in ways that were not intentionally supporting these things moving forward.

INTRODUCTION

Doctor, the same is true for you. Your energy, your time, and your overhead are being sucked away on massive amounts of patients; only about 20 percent of which are actually accepting work, and not all of those are accepting the full case. You are exhausting yourself and this book is your destiny moment!

Doctor John recently reached out to me while at the end of his rope. John ran a bread-and-butter practice. By all accounts, his practice, in terms of numbers, did better than many dental practices in the US. His adjusted production was $1.5 million, or about $125,000 a month. John's collections, unfortunately, were about 85 percent of that adjusted number.

Including his part-timers, John had fourteen employees just to be able to handle the endless amounts of patients that passed through his office, filling his days. With payroll and the money he spent on marketing, his overhead left a razor-thin profit. He always worried about covering payroll, paying other bills, and paying himself. Every day, the moment he walked through the door, it was like a gun went off—and the race started. All day he played catchup, running from operatory to operatory, spending the bare minimum of time with patients, trying to talk them into single unit crowns and fillings, inevitably listening to them talk about insurance and how they couldn't afford it. He never felt his compensation was commensurate with the energy he put into his practice.

As bizarre as it seems, when John contacted me, he was seeing ninety new patients a month, and the first question out of his mouth was, Sean, can you help me get more new patients? In John's view the only way to grow was by adding more new patients, even though his current patient load had him at the end of his rope. He wasn't seeing the reality that more new patients meant more of everything else: more payroll, more hours, more days added to the schedule, and he wasn't seeing the heart condition or at least the complete burnout that he was inevitably headed for.

Now, compare Daniel, who I worked with for about six years. Daniel's situation had major differences to John's—even though the demographics were socioeconomically similar, his practice looked very different. Daniel had four employees: two assistants, one hygienist, and one front desk person. Daniel tracked his production at his fees, not at the insurance adjusted fees, and in doing so, knew exactly where his true collection rate landed. Daniel was producing $1.8 million a year, or about $150,000 a month, at his fees and his collection rates averaged 95 percent. Acceptance of the treatment presented was considered the basis for success and tracked meticulously. Tracking these areas in this way provided information about when or if he could drop the safety net of in-network insurance relationships and how he might adjust his financial policies. On an average day, Daniel served between seven and fifteen patients, including the hygiene patients. Daniel shaped his practice to create value at the highest level for the services that he performed. He performed comprehensive diagnoses and comprehensive treatments, and he did this by focusing on implementing my strategies.

The clock rarely hounded Daniel, so he developed meaningful relationships with his patients. His team controlled the environment, the patients, and the results, and they were very confident in their job roles. He never felt that he failed to contribute, and his pay felt like a well-earned reward for all the work he put in. When Daniel retired from dentistry, he sold his practice for nearly 90 percent of the previous twelve months collections, when the average selling price was 65 percent of the same. This book lays out strategies to help you be more like Daniel—and less like John—regardless of where you are in the current journey of your practice.

After implementing the strategies detailed in this book, your dental practice will multiply its revenue without constantly chasing after endless amounts of new patients.

Throughout the following pages, I'm going to use the word *sales*, and I'm going to use *sales* interchangeably with the term *treatment acceptance* and *value creation*; all three terms are interchangeable. Sales is treatment acceptance, and treatment acceptance is nothing more than learning how to create value for the products and the services that you provide: there's nothing unethical or immoral about it. There's a reason that sales is a profession and that professional sales people are the highest paid people on the planet. Good sales practices can help you provide much needed health care to the many neglectful patients.

I'm going to go step-by-step to show you how to implement the things that will make a difference in your practice. In the first chapter, I ask that you be willing to change your thinking and talk about why and how that is imperative to your results. Then, I teach you why people buy and how important it is not only to understand but also to believe the real reason people buy. We're going to talk about how you can create value for your patients, your team, your dentistry, and your time, and the specific role for each team member in your practice. This book covers how to track the implementation of these principles, and finally, I want to show you how to coach the process, like Daniel, so that you can prioritize and implement the strategies that ensure success.

CHALLENGE YOUR OWN THINKING

You must take a pause from running room to room and think for a moment: when it comes to marketing dollars, you know that your pockets aren't as deep as the corporate practices. You also know that even if they were as deep, the burnout factor would come sooner rather than later, if your growth only centers around marketing and days/hours added to your schedule. So then, how can your practice grow without massively growing the number of new patients or continually adding days and hours to your schedule? There are definitely things you'll have to do differently, but since you can't outdo the immovable corporate giants, you must outserve and outperform them—but it all starts with outthinking them!

Be, Do, Have

Stephen Covey, Tony Robbins, Zig Ziglar, and many others have all talked about the concept of "be do have". Here's my view: How you're *be*ing in your mind will determine the things that you'll *do*, and what you do determines what you get to *have* (the results that you're after). My over two-decades experience has made it clear that focusing on the reality of be-do-have, in that order, can mean the difference between success and failure; it's the one sticking point that can explain the *why* of a faltering dental business. Anytime you're implementing new systems in your business—or, frankly, any change in your life—you should come at it from be-do-have, in that order.

So you want to implement systems in your practice that allow you to be more successful without relying solely on the never-ending chase for massive amounts of new patients. If you skip the *be* part and go straight to *do* (implementation), then you're not going to have the results you hoped for because the implementation will never stay engrained! Changing tactics (what you do) alone is not enough: all change must begin with a changed mindset. A changed mindset is a deliberate process that ends up determining what we do and whether or not it lasts. It is unfortunate that dentistry is full of offices that implement new systems only to have them last a few days or weeks before they magically disappear. Why?

Probably for the same reason that people look for the mythical "do this" diet to lose weight . . . it's just easier than changing the mindset required to eat right and control weight—it's just human nature!

For example, we've all announced, or know someone who has announced, "I'm going to start working out." They go to the gym only a few times or on a few runs before the workout routine is forgotten. Again, because they didn't change the way they were thinking. They simply went straight to doing. Pretty soon they skip one day, then another, then a whole chunk of time passes, and they are back where they started.

You must be the person who enjoys going to the gym, not the person that plans to go to the gym, nor the person that has merely written "gym" a few times on his calendar. Who hasn't skipped the gym, even though it's written on the calendar? If you skip enough times, you won't get results. "Health enthusiasts," as the name implies, are enthusiastic about their health; they have the right mindset (being), they rarely skip a workout (doing), and by looking at them, you can see the results (having).

When changing any behavior, people focus almost entirely on the doing, not the mindset required to keep the doing in place. Yet the mindset is where the long-term change takes place. Thirteen months before my first marathon,

I had never run more than 3 miles. My friend and long-term client, Dr. Ellis Stonehocker, said that once we sign up, there is no backing out. I had no earthly idea how I was going to train enough to ever run 26.2 miles. But what got me through to the marathon finish line, what got me through that thirteen months of training, wasn't all the running, but where I went and remained mentally. As luck would have it a month after committing, I was shot . . . in the head. And, among other things, my vocal cords were paralyzed, which made for interesting breathing challenges and freight-train type noises as I ran. But it became the thing that connected me to my training. Whether it was 3 a.m. or 9 p.m., my training time was my proving to myself that being shot and not able to speak was NOT going to define me. I would miss meals before I missed training—literally!

If you do something only to do it, there's no mental connection to what's behind what you do. Then when the going gets tough (and it most certainly will), it's very easy to stop doing the right things, and we've all been there. So, before taking a single step, you must think through your journey: not only the itinerary but the motive behind each step (Why am I doing this?).

"I'm going back to the gym" is not a sufficient mindset, no matter the resolve with which it's said. You must become the person that enjoys going to the gym by attaching a motive behind it.

In 2019 my business partner and I were challenged to accomplish a 70.3 Ironman. For those who don't know, a Half Ironman is a 1.2-mile swim, a 56-mile bike and a 13.1-mile half marathon at the end. I thought about this long and hard. I was fifty-one at the time and my business partner was a vibrant thirty-six. I knew from past experience that if I were to attempt it, I had to get a motive behind such an accomplishment—had to get my *be* or I would never even survive the training. I couldn't find one motive . . . and yet agreed anyway. When it was time to begin training, I struggled. Every morning was a gripe session between us: "What are we doing at 5:00 a.m. in the lake? This water is freezing! This is a terrible idea! What were we thinking?" As you can imagine, it was drudgery. Somewhere in that first two weeks I found my be.

My motive was to be able to competitively come close to my partner. How cool would I feel if at fifty—when I could at least hang with the young guy. From that point I began to look forward to the training. My wife even picked up on it and would ask, "How are you keeping up?" Every morning became a competition. It became contagious and I saw him pushing; if he skipped, I could tell he felt like I was getting ahead of him. After months and months of training, it felt great to accomplish 70.3 miles, but honestly, while I know his motivation was different from mine, for me it felt better knowing I beat the young guy.

Having a successful dental business is the same. You know that you, and more importantly your team, will have to do things much differently. You must get connected to the right mindset and get your team connected to the right mindset before and during change. Most skip over the be and jump right to the do, but if it's skipped, change never lasts! And if you and I are going to learn how you can increase your revenue without increasing the days worked or the number of new patients that you're seeing, then you must change the way you think. Right now, before reading the rest of this book, begin focusing on what mindset you need—who you need to be—in order to implement the things that you need to do so that you get to have the results that you're after. I sometimes think of it this way: What is the motive that will carry me through the unforeseen challenges, the challenges that I *know* will make it easy to abandon the process. Be, do, have: a mindset, or state of being, with the right focus will naturally do the right things and have what it seeks.

Identify Your References

To locate the correct mindset, we must first figure out what makes up that mindset before really going after what you need to do.

For several years, I had the privilege of working with Tony Robbins, a world-renowned motivational speaker and bestselling author. He has written many books and spoken extensively on the concept of beliefs and what makes up our beliefs. He gives a fantastic and simple explanation of how references shape our beliefs:

When you and I experience or learn something new, an idea is formed. That idea is like a loosely floating cloud. Then, through more experiences, knowledge, education, or other influences, we gain references that either support the idea or perhaps distinguish it. The more references, the more the idea solidifies until the cloud becomes solid like a tabletop. A solid belief based on enough supporting references can become fact in our minds. The problem (or opportunity) is that the references we gain are all individual and depend on our own circumstances and experiences. This is a massive part of what makes up our mindset, and, I can't repeat it enough, how we are *being* in our mind determines what we do.

Belief can explain why people from the same area and time can turn out differently—also, why the two dentists from the introduction, John and Daniel, can practice in a similar demographic but have very different results.

Several years ago, I watched an interview of Dr. Ben Carson before he ran for president (Carson 2010). Carson was a neurosurgeon for over three decades before becoming a politician.

And it just so happens that he is from a city in Michigan where I've had many clients. In the interview, Carson said that the neighborhood he grew up in was poor and dangerous—most Americans would lock their doors and roll up their windows if they had to drive through it. But he says that there were plenty of people who were smarter and more talented than him, yet he became a neurosurgeon while many of those same smart and gifted people never made it out of the old neighborhood. The difference? His beliefs. His mother instilled in him the belief that he could become whatever he desired. She pushed him as a youngster to read anything and everything he could get his hands on so that he could discover his purpose.

Ben Carson went on to say that many of the people still in his old neighborhood never had that limitless belief—their belief was the opposite: I'm not smart enough, I don't have what it takes, and I'm trapped in this neighborhood; there's no way I'm getting out. He went on to explain that even if some tried to grow and get out, others would dash their hope and say, "It isn't possible. We can't get out." The only difference between me and them, Carson said, was and is my belief.

Beliefs are the number one thing that make up your mindset and the great news is that *you can choose your beliefs*. Books, Google, social media: the possibilities for gaining information are endless. Your beliefs don't have to be formed *only* by your own experiences; you can consciously choose where you get information as well as what information you seek out. So, you must be willing to challenge your beliefs by gaining as much information as possible that gives you references to support an idea becoming solid, like a tabletop. Check every idea before you accept it—be responsible and choose your references; otherwise, your beliefs will be formed on wrong or misguided premises, and the energy you expend doing things at the direction of a faulty belief cannot be returned.

When deciding what to read or listen to, seek out sources that support the belief you wish to cultivate and the success that you're trying to achieve. Don't listen, watch, or read media that merely flows in and out of your life, failing to monitor the references that solidify and form the basis of a belief. Choose the references that you believe will support the change and growth you are after.

Instilling not only the will but also the method for challenging your beliefs is the essence of what I'm talking about. I once held the belief that people buy things based on money. It took nearly starving to gain enough references to learn how to truly create value. In the next chapter, we talk about being willing to challenge entrenched beliefs and the value challenging beliefs creates.

Shift Your Mindset

People protect their current beliefs and mindset even when their business isn't successful; our thinking becomes about why other beliefs are wrong and so abandoning our current mindset is never worth it. We're convinced that doing things differently would get the same result or worse: that patients will not buy it. So, why even try? There's always an excuse to avoid the discomfort of change.

When I first began a career in the dental industry, I was so excited that I knew something that dentistry didn't. My first career was in telecommunications, where I was a sales executive and sales trainer. When coming to dentistry, I realized that I took for granted the principles of sales: sales is about asking open-ended questions and value, not price. All salespeople learn these foundational principles. I was like a kid in a candy store when I realized that sales is treatment acceptance and that dentistry didn't know it or implement it. It was like I was the only one who knew how to speak a language that was foreign to dentistry.

As I mentioned earlier, I was so eager to help that for years I would go anywhere, anytime to help anyone, yet I was killing myself. All my energy was being drained by clients who weren't implementing my strategies. I realized something really did have to change if I was going to have any quality to the rest of my life and at the same time make any kind of impact in dentistry. I came to the conclusion that my mindset would have to change. I discovered that I had a belief that hard work equaled success. Up to that point I had never really differentiated between hard work that was going somewhere versus hard work that was wasted time. Work was work and it was necessary for success. When consulting dentists, all my focus was on work—on giving—and yet there were some who refused to receive! So, I asked myself, what is the difference between the clients who implemented my systems and excelled and the clients who didn't implement at all? The lesson about the importance of mindset finally hit home for me: mindset determines results, therefore, success.

The clients that succeeded weren't attached to beliefs that prevented them from implementing my strategies; they were willing to challenge and even let me challenge the beliefs that held them back, and so they accumulated both good results and business success. Unfortunately, some clients just had a set of beliefs that held them back, and they were entrenched in those beliefs. The comfort of staying with those beliefs outweighed the discomfort of their lack of success. With these clients, it was emotionally draining. My time wasn't spent implementing strategies but convincing them that the strategies were worth implementing—I realized that I couldn't do anything for them. So, I made my first destiny-defining decision: I was no longer going to increase my time away from my family for clients unwilling to challenge their self-defeating beliefs.

I created a client-vetting process at The Crabtree Group. First, before we accept a client we do an initial broad consult where we ascertain that the client is willing to challenge their own thinking; otherwise, we'll not spend our time with them. Second, I got rid of about 50 percent of our clients, ones who weren't willing to overcome their deep-seeded beliefs and who weren't implementing my strategies that would get them results. Our results at The Crabtree Group skyrocketed from then on. On average, our clients as a whole experience 48 percent growth.

The moral of this chapter is, do not kill yourself attempting to make a set of beliefs work: be willing to mold your mindset with references and beliefs that support your success.

Learn (and Believe) Why People Buy

This may be one of the shortest chapters in this book, yet it is the most powerful and most important.

As a dentist, it's unlikely that you've spent any time learning the concepts behind why people buy. And I get it, you've spent a ridiculous amount of time, money, and energy learning the clinical aspects of dentistry. So, where are you getting your business advice then? Most likely from other people who have never learned sales—namely, other dentists. Their advice was formed by their experiences or handed down from other dentists, who learned their business practices from the previous generation who also never learned sales. It's unfortunate that awesome clinical skills have zero bearing on having a successful dental business. Now, there's obvious wisdom that can be learned from past successful dental business owners, and from your colleagues, but your dental business is most likely built on nonbusiness practices and in many ways sabotaging your success.

Why Do People Buy?

The belief in why people buy is the number one issue that comes into play in any sort of sales situation. Your belief in why people buy anything will determine what you do and the results you get to have.

Learning and believing are two very different things. Learning conceptually why people buy something doesn't mean that you'll implement it in all situations. For an unwavering belief to form, you must have enough references that develop the ideas you're learning into a solid belief (see the cloud and tabletop analogy from the last chapter).

Specifically, your beliefs about patient treatment acceptance are holding you back. These beliefs are supported by references, and references come in the form of things we've heard, read, watched, interpreted from past experiences, and the like. As a dentist, you've probably only encountered references about treatment acceptance from other dentists or from your interpretation of your own experience with patients. It goes without saying, but these can be the worst possible places to gain references.

For example, when you present treatment to a patient, they're never going to consciously think through what you've said and analyze their feelings about it: they'll simply ask about the money. When you tell a patient that he needs a crown, he isn't going to say, "Doc, you know, I know you're telling me I need this crown, but honestly it doesn't hurt and it's just not something I see value in. But, that 84-inch flat screen TV I've been wanting for my man cave . . . I see value in that." The patient is likely only to remark that the dental procedure is way too expensive: "I can't afford that." Or ask, "How much does my insurance cover?" When you hear this from your patients over and over and over again, you begin to develop references that what you hear your patients say must be true. You begin to believe that "my fees must be too high" or "my patients cannot afford the dentistry they need."

Accordingly, when you hear the same patient experiences from your colleagues, who have experienced this for years and years, your references are reinforced—it must be true that people buy because of money. *This belief is absolutely not true.*

It's the perfect example of what was described in the first chapter, a belief that you *must* be willing to challenge if you desire success. If you're willing to challenge that belief, then you must begin to seek out references for why people buy that support that success. For example, go google *Why do people buy?* and begin the search for new references. The first result that populated for me was a tenet of sales theory: people buy products or services according to emotional needs or wants and then justify their purchases logically.

When you understand the emotional reasons why people buy, you can connect with people on that level—their level—and you'll then have tremendous power to provide your patients with what they want. Patients won't only get what they want but also appreciate you for providing the product or service.

This concept was a tough one for me to get early on in my career. I began seeking out the right references and developing my own reference system that led to forming the right beliefs. You have to do the same if you ever want to change your thinking. So, go read other books, listen to experts outside your field, and take someone successful out for lunch.

Throughout the rest of this chapter, I'm going to start you off and give you some references through stories, stats, and other examples, but you can't stop there: go make your own!

It's Not about Price, It's about Value

As an undergraduate student at Middle Tennessee State University, I took a class called the Psychology of Consumer Buying Behavior. I still remember my professor walking into this huge auditorium, wearing jeans with the knees blown out and a cowboy hat that failed to contain his Einstein-looking hair. To complete the look, he was smoking a pipe. While handing out the syllabus, the very first thing out of his mouth was this: "Nobody that you have ever known, or ever will know, including yourself, has ever, or will ever, buy anything based strictly on cost." He paused for this to sink in, then he said, "We all buy based on value. It's emotional and it's individual, then we justify our purchase based on some logical reason."

I thought, I'm in the wrong class; this is the stupidest thing I've ever heard. As a college student, everything I do is because of money. Every week, my goal was to squeeze a week's worth of food—with beer money left over—out of fifty dollars. And I was good at it by the way: living off ramen noodles and tuna fish, foraging for discounts and good deals.

But it wasn't until later that I absorbed the sales concept taught by my professor. My first real job out of college was in the telecommunications industry, when cell phones were in their infancy.

I was a professional salesperson for a new, small company called Cellular One.

As you know, most cellular carriers would take a loss on the cell phone because they would make up the cost over the life of the service contract. Cellular One was a franchise company; back then the cellular service regions were by coverage areas, serviced by a single given company. If a person drove into another service area, another company's domain, the person is roaming, and—if you remember—roaming charges were expensive and as much as $3.00 per minute. The whole system was confusing and overcomplicated for companies.

The phones were also extremely expensive. Motorola made the first cell phones on the market. For us, the phones cost about $1,250. We could only afford to take a small loss on the phones, so we were selling them for $1,150 each, a considerable purchase for a company looking for multiple lines. I would give my sales pitch to CEOs, who would inevitably ask, Sean, can't I drive an hour down the road and get a hundred of the same phones for $150 each? I would admit that you could and if I were him, I would probably make the drive and do just that.

Every time I got this question, I couldn't lie to them, that wouldn't be right, and yet, how the heck was I going to make any money? I concluded that I wasn't a very good salesperson.

Learn (and Believe) Why People Buy

I believed that all decisions were ultimately determined by money. Through hard knocks, this job made me realize what my professor taught was true. It's about value!

It took losing sales left and right until I had finally hit the end of my rope. I was making no money, so I concluded that sales was definitely not for me; however, eventually something interesting happened. After talking to me, companies would just drive an hour down the road and buy numerous cellular lines, and then they would inevitably need all kinds of service. With batteries shot, antenna issues, roaming problems, guess who they called when "an hour down the road" wouldn't solve their problem? I was spending a ridiculous amount of time helping all these companies; I, of course, made zero money doing it. But I was making great relationships and getting deep into these companies, and occasionally they would add lines with me. One day I was helping the purchasing department of a particular company (for the umpteenth time) when the CEO walked. He said, "Sean, I appreciate how you take care of us. I really wish I had known the difference in working with you"—versus *an hour down the road*—"We will never buy anywhere else. The way you take care of us is well worth the difference in price." After I thanked him, I asked if he would mind putting that in writing.

Previously, I was only comparing our hardware prices with my competitor. I never considered that the service that was required with the cell phones could be more valuable than price. That I was value. Companies needed not only servicing but also customer service and constant training. And then I learned: my understanding of sales changed.

So I began seeking out compliments from other companies that I took care of so that I had the opportunity to ask, would you mind putting that in writing? If I had another CEO contact you, would you be willing to communicate that? And inevitably they did. I built a portfolio according to that value. That's when my sales took off. That's when I really started selling three and four hundred lines: record sales at the time. But again, it's because I learned the concept that it's not about price, it's about value.

Let me help with a reference that I'll bet you've seen before in your office; it might be possible you've been looking at it another way. Recently, I was visiting a practice doing what I call an *opportunity analysis*. Basically, in addition to gaining all the necessary information on the practice vitals, I visit the practice in person to see them in action, as well as visit with individual staff members and the doctors. While observing a new patient visit, I saw the doctor walk in for the exam. After some small talk and a comprehensive exam, she walked the patient through the intraoral camera shots and explained a crack and how this was going to need a crown. She explained all the bad things that could happen if not crowned and how Murphy's Law would make sure that it happened at the worst possible time. She very thoroughly explained what a crown entailed and asked if he had any questions.

She then asked about his summer vacation plans, and he talked of taking the family to Mexico and so forth. She explained that he certainly wanted to prevent an issue from happening while in Mexico. After more small talk, the patient was escorted to the front. There, the front desk walked him through the treatment plan, but before she could finish, he interrupted, "How much does my insurance cover"; after her response he said, "That's way too high. I can't afford that. I'll call you back."

After the patient walked out, I asked the front desk what she thought happened. She explained that patients in this area just don't have any money. I ran to the window just as the patient opened the door to his fully loaded GMC Denali of the same year! Clearly the patient sees value in a $65,000 vehicle and a trip to Mexico but no value for a crown that, by the way, wasn't hurting! Again, you'll never hear a patient say, "You know, it's just that I see value in a new flat screen TV, whereas I don't see value in a crown"; clients will simply say, "That's too much." All the more reason that you need to believe that it's not about price, it's about value!

It's Not about Logic, It's about Emotion

Buying decisions are emotionally based. Every person on earth, you and I, consumers, and your patients, all base every decision on emotional reasons. While money driving sales was a belief I had to overcome, the emotional component of sales was a given for me, not only because of my training in sales and in college but because psychologically to me it makes sense. I naturally thought that this revelation was common knowledge.

When I came to dentistry with this knowledge, I saw a field where this was not at all common or practiced. This void is one of the exciting things that brought me to and got me to stay in dentistry. I can't tell you how unbelievably exciting it was to come into an industry with knowledge that I found literally not one dentist or team that I encountered understood or implemented. Even today I still find dentists and teams who don't understand this, and I've actually had some who try and convince me that it's only women who make emotional buying decisions. Look, it doesn't matter that you are a dentist and your patient is an engineer, you and your patient and every other human on earth involve emotions in *every* decision. Even if you consider yourself fully devoid of emotions, they still play a role in every decision you make!

This concept of why people buy takes me back to my first psychology class. The pleasure-pain principle is one of the first things you learn in psychology. The decisions we make are inevitably rooted in the need to escape some kind of pain or get to some kind of pleasure. We make our decisions to buy according to some sort of emotional pain that we're trying to get out of or some sort of emotional pleasure that we're trying to get to.

There are many references out there that support how important our emotions are in decision-making. One example is a study done by the University of Iowa's neurology department (Bechara 2004). It found that people with brain damage to a specific part of the prefrontal cortex, the part that controls feelings and emotions, are incapable of making decisions. The study supports the emotional decision-making you encounter every day in your hygiene or operative chairs. Buying decisions are emotionally based, and the only way value can be created is to tie the dentistry needed to alleviate the emotional pain or increase the pleasure of the patient. When you take into account that most needed dentistry isn't felt, or actively hurting, you can see how unbelievably vital it is to get this concept.

So, how to be successful at sales is to first understand that buying is determined by individual value and always emotionally driven.

GETTING CLEAR ON HOW TO CREATE VALUE

Now, you understand the most important pieces of this book: (1) the value of changing your own thinking as well as (2) understanding and believing the real reason people buy is emotional, individual, and based on value. Being armed with these principles can help make the next hurdle easy to overcome. It is the single biggest distinction perhaps ever in your practice! It is at the very core of the how-to of increasing revenue without adding massive amounts of new patients to your practice.

Redefine the Exam

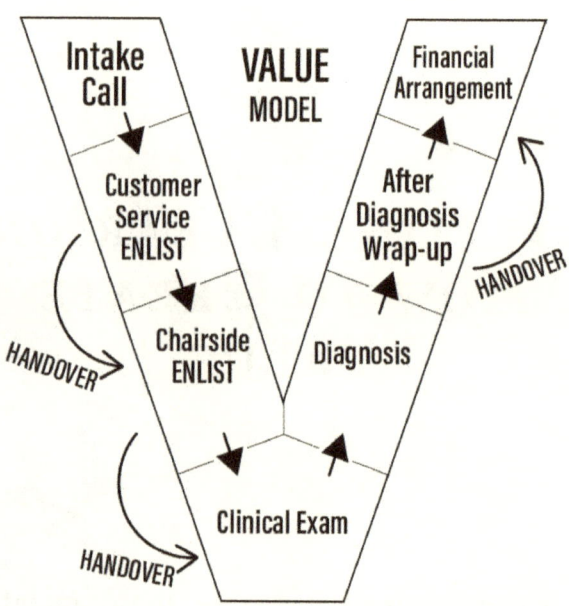

The seven stages of the Value Model. Chapter 3 covers the bottom of the V, the chairside ENLIST, the clinical exam, and diagnosis, as well as the after diagnosis wrap-up. Chapter 4 completes the model: the intake call, the customer service ENLIST, and the financial arrangement.

Doctor, you and your team must redefine the term "comprehensive exam." In the past the comprehensive examination was defined in specific clinical terms, in the mouth.

Understanding the previous chapters means that you and your team must redefine it. Moving forward, this exam cannot be considered comprehensive unless it first includes an examination of the heart and mind that makes decisions for the mouth—and this happens with your team, specifically your hygienist or assistant before you see the patient!

Your assistants and hygienists need to know that basically 50 percent of a comprehensive exam is driven by them before you enter the room. Remember, you and I and the patient perceive value emotionally and subjectively, so before you, as the doctor, can provide value, you must know how the individual, the patient, sees value. Your assistant or your hygienist must listen for what the patient values, appealing to the patient's heart and mind, and relay that information in a handover to you when you enter the room.

As captain of the ship, Doctor, you've got to do a couple of things. First, I would challenge your whole team to get on the same page. Because the first half of the exam is so vital and because it is performed by them, your team must also understand and believe the reasons why people buy. The whole team must understand that value in the heart and mind determines what happens with the mouth.

Second, redefine the exam. If you don't have the heart-and-mind information handed over to you, you can only complete half the exam. This information is necessary to direct what happens clinically. You must draw a hard line with your team and convey not just the importance but the necessity of this information. So, Doctor, you must redefine a comprehensive exam to include (1) what's going on clinically in the mouth and (2) what's important to the heart and mind of the patient who owns and makes decisions for the mouth.

You should expect a handover from your hygienist or assistant about the findings of the examination of the heart and mind. These findings, plus the clinical exam, will allow you to make a diagnosis. If you only have one or the other, then you don't have a comprehensive exam and you don't have enough information to make a diagnosis.

If you constantly find yourself presenting several options for treatment, then you clearly only have the clinical half of the examination performed. I have run into this for years with doctors, explaining to me how they diagnose either conservatively or aggressively. If you're having to insert your views into a treatment plan, you clearly don't have enough information to present. This isn't about you! There's no question that certain cases can clinically be handled in different ways, but when you run into that, before

Getting Clear on How to Create Value

you present multiple treatment options, think about this: when you know what's important to the patient's heart and mind, a single option will clearly present itself. And that treatment is neither conservative nor aggressive, it's the best.

I'm not suggesting that you shouldn't explain options; there's nothing inherently wrong with that. But there's clearly only one best treatment and you should explain why based on everything discovered in the comprehensive exam. You're in the same situation as any other professional who uses his or her knowledge, experience, and training to diagnose. When you have central heating and air issues, the HVAC professional takes a (clinical) look at your unit; similarly, in some cases, there may be more than one option. The smart professional realizes that to recommend the best plan, a simple look at the unit isn't enough. Your emotional concerns as the homeowner must be examined also before the diagnosis can be made. If this point isn't realized, then chapter 2 is out the window.

This entire book could be written on this topic alone. I cannot stress its importance enough. It is happening all over America in dental practices right now. Patients are released to the front desk to walk through financials on several different treatment plans and the doctor is expecting the patient to accept the ideal plan. No matter how awesome your team member in the front is, she cannot close an optimal treatment plan when there's not one but several. All she can do is go over the dollars required for each treatment and watch as the patient becomes overwhelmed with the information and leaves to think about it, or at best, chooses the least expensive treatment.

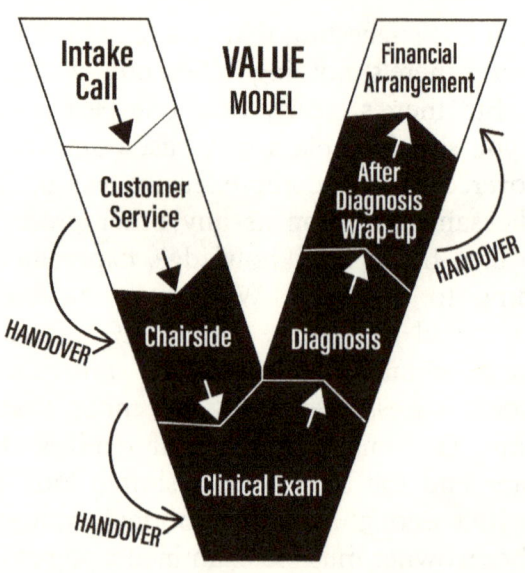

To get the full picture of how to create value, it's important to see it visually at work in your practice. I created the Value Model as a representation of how a new patient enters your realm, beginning at the top left with the intake call and culminating at the top right with the financial arrangement. This is the entire process, start to finish. Each step builds, supports, and leads to the next, ultimately making it as easy as possible for the patient to accept the dental work they want and need.

All seven stages will be covered, but this chapter is specific to the centrepiece of creating value and how it really happens in the room with the patient—beginning chairside. From there to the clinical exam through the diagnosis to the after diagnosis wrap-up, as well as what happens in-between, called handovers. This is the middle of the entire sales continuum, and where the rubber meets the road when it comes to value creation.

Before the process can be put into the above steps of the Value Model, we must be crystal clear on the process itself . . . the actual process of creating value. Let me introduce you to ENLIST.

ENLIST

Since Newton discovered the law of gravity, it has been taught hundreds of different ways throughout history to make the concept easy to learn and understand. Similarly, value creation is not a new concept and throughout history has been taught many different ways for the same reasons. Most all training is broken down in a five to seven step acronym. Mine is called E N L I S T.

ENLIST stands for:

E—engage the patient

N—'nquire or inquire (that quirk should help make it memorable)

L—listen, for the emotion

I—intensify the emotional pain

S—save the patient with the benefits of the treatment

T—trial close

Remember your patients are consumers. As such, they are as ignorant of dentistry as I am of automotive or you are of another industry. So unless I hear a knock in my engine or your patients feels pain in a tooth, value is not automatically seen. ENLIST allows you to create value for the needed work, whether it's felt or not.

Engage the Patient

Engaging the patient sets the stage; the ease of the following five steps depends on its success. Since we now know people buy for individual and emotional reasons, we have to find out what those specific reasons are for each patient. The only way we can do that is to ask open-ended questions to the patient. The engagement step sets up the ability to ask these questions, and without it, patients won't play along, or they'll give you the deer in the headlights look.

There are two very specific aims that you're trying to accomplish with engagement: you want the patient to understand (1) how asking these probing questions benefits them and (2) how it benefits them that they should be comfortable enough to open their heart to you.

Here's an example of engagement: "Mr. Patient, I don't know if you saw our vision statement out front, but it's something that all of us here at ABC Dental take very seriously. And basically what it says is that we're committed to serving you at the highest level possible. The only way that I can serve you at that level is to get some information from you. You might not have encountered these questions in a dental office before, so if you need to take a moment to really give me a heartfelt kind of answer, please take all the time you need."

Okay, that sets the stage. Your hygienist or your assistant will perform this step for existing and new patients. While engaging the patient, your hygienist or your assistant will be looking for verbal or body language clues from the patient. They should always ask themselves: According to these cues, do I believe this patient understands (a) how it benefits them that I'm about to ask these questions and (b) how it benefits them that they're comfortable enough to share what's on their heart?

Now, the first step has been performed and your team members are confident that its two points have been accomplished. Having listened and watched for verbal and body language clues, your hygienist or your assistant is confident that the patient understands the benefit to them on both points. Now, your team is ready to begin the next steps of ENLIST, specifically the next three: N, L, and I.

After setting the stage by engaging the patient, your hygienist or your assistant are going to cycle through the next two steps—inquiring and listening, inquiring and listening, inquiring and listening—until they reach the emotional value, then intensifying it before bringing you in. Doctor, you'll complete the clinical part of the examination, give a diagnosis, and exit, leaving your hygienist or your assistant to wrap up. The wrap-up is in the last two parts: saving the patient with the benefits and the trial close.

As with any sales process, inquiring, inquiring, inquiring to discover what's most important to the patient is vital. If you begin inquiring without the benefit of engaging the patient first, they won't understand where the benefit lies. In other words, they'll think you're asking questions for you and not for them. In this

Getting Clear on How to Create Value

case, they're much more likely to tell you what they think you want to hear or simply to give tooth-related answers, neither of which you're after.

Remember, your assistant isn't looking for tooth-related answers—you can find out what's going on with the teeth by performing a clinical exam. Answers from the heart and mind are what you're after, initially. Emotionally how they feel about their smile. Are they embarrassed, self-conscience, or perhaps looking to become more confident about their smile?

"So, Mr. Patient, what's most important to you about your smile?" You're looking for an emotional answer, so inquire and listen, inquire and listen, inquire and listen until you get that emotional answer.

How do I recognize an emotional answer? It's simple. The patient's answer fits into one of the following two sentences:

- The most important thing to this patient about their smile is feeling _____.
- The most important thing to this patient about their smile is not feeling _____.

Healthy is not a feeling, but there's something behind the word, so keep inquiring. The patient wants to feel confident, attractive, or dazzling, or the patient does not want to feel embarrassed, self-conscious, or ashamed. These are sentiments about their smile that you're looking for, so you're going to inquire and listen, until the patient opens up to you. Over the years, I've learned that inquiring is simply a matter of repeating the question but changing the wording and emphasis.

Here's an inquiring-and-listening scenario:

"Mr. Patient, what's most important to you about your smile?"

"I'd like it to be white and straight."

"What's most important to you about having a white and straight smile?"

"I think everyone wants a nice smile."

"What's most important to you about having a nice smile?"

"I'd feel much more confident about myself."

Continue to inquire and listen, ask open-ended questions, and wait for the response that reveals the emotional value (in the above scenario, the emotional value is that the patient wants to be confident). Once you get the feel, you can aim to elicit more than one emotional value from a patient. And once you hear the emotional-value answer, you can proceed to the next step—intensification.

Intensification is the step where you allow the patient to really feel that pain emotionally, to really connect with the negativity its causing in their lives. This step is achieved by proceeding with the back-and-forth with the patient by asking past, present, and future questions. After twenty-two years of training hygienists and assistants, a simplified version can sound like this:

Inquiring and Listening

Inquiring. "So, Mr. Patient, what's most important to you about your smile?"

Listening. "You know, I want straight and white teeth."

Inquiring. "What's most important to you about that?"

Listening. "Well, I'm embarrassed by these two front teeth. They're crooked and this right one is larger than the left."

Intensification

Past Question. "Oh, my goodness, how long have you felt embarrassed about that?"

"Um, honestly, since I was about eighteen years old."

Present Question. "Wow, that's been affecting you for quite awhile. How is feeling embarrassed currently affecting you?"

"I'm not as outgoing as I once was. I really notice it when I'm in business and social type settings: I tend to cover my mouth when I smile and never let people see me laugh really big."

Future Question. "So, I guess I have one last question: How long are you going to continue to feel embarrassed before we do something about it?"

"I have no idea what it's going to take, but I'm ready, I'm really ready."

The above came from a patient nearly word-for-word. The patient has already accepted that he needs treatment before the clinical exam. Now, when you walk in as the doctor, the patient is eager for the treatment solution and they only need to know what it is. Think about how opposite that is from the way it's currently being done in your office: right now, when you walk in, you perform the exam, and because you have nothing to go on, you have to make a diagnosis based on a crack, decay, or some sort of problem—fix and repair dentistry only. Then you give a diagnosis, but because it doesn't hurt, you or your team spend time trying to convince the patient why they need it.

These aren't questions about teeth but questions about feelings . . . about teeth. And it's only the feeling that can be intensified. The goal isn't to intensify about the teeth. Don't ask the patient, "How long have you had those crooked teeth?" but "How long have you felt embarrassed about your teeth?" The fact that the teeth are crooked isn't the problem, it's the cause of the problem. The problem is feeling embarrassed. That's what you're trying to help with and that's what should be intensified.

Because the problem has been identified as embarrassment, you're free to diagnose everything that might affect that emotion and present all the options in terms of, in this case, embarrassment. In other words, you're not limited to the patient only seeing value in certain teeth. Everything they need done can now be presented in terms of eliminating or preventing embarrassment.

Remember, Doctor, the first four steps—engagement, inquiring, listening, and intensifying—are done by your hygienist or your assistant before you step into the room. Only once the hygienist has asked the patient the past, present, and future questions—and the emotional value has been intensified—is it time for you to step into the room.

The Handover

At this point, Doctor, the work has already been done for you. Before you arrive in the operatory, your hygienist or your assistant has engaged the patient, inquired and listened, and found and intensified that pain—the emotional value—with past, present, and future questions. So, when you walk in, all this has been done for you. As you enter, you'll be informed of the findings of the first half of the exam—in other words, your hygienist will hand over the information. Now it's your opportunity to do the clinical exam and to base your diagnosis on the findings of both exams. Remember, Doctor, you must sincerely understand the first half of the exam, because your expertise and understanding are needed to couple the clinical exam with the emotional value to ultimately provide value to the patient. Armed with this information, you're now fully free to diagnose everything that might be related to the patient's emotional value. This is why it's important to the patient.

Of course, in the above example, there are two teeth mentioned, but anything else that you see—anterior, posterior—can now be filtered through what's most important to the patient. Now you aren't simply fixing teeth, you're fixing the patient's embarrassment from this point and into the future.

Patients won't accept recommended clinical work unless, or until, they see value in it. In addition, you must always remind your team about the significance of the first half of the exam, and you must constantly remind yourself to listen carefully to the handover, ensuring the information passed on informs your exam going forward. So, armed with belief in your team and in the process before you enter the room, how might a handover go?

"Doctor, this is Ms. Patient. Ms. Patient and I have had a great conversation. More than anything else, she wants the confidence that can only come from a straight white smile. You know, she's been telling me that since she was eighteen, she's always been self-conscious about her smile. Especially now that her work depends on making sales in real estate. It's affecting her ability to be her natural, confident self because she's constantly trying to hide her smile. She's really ready to get something done here."

This is your opportunity to say, "Great, now let me take a look."

You go in and do your clinical examination. Once you've finished your clinical examination, present your diagnosis—"I look forward to seeing you next time"—and leave the room, off to the next patient.

The After Diagnosis Wrap-Up

Now that the emotional value has been intensified and the diagnosis made (and you've left the room), your hygienist or your assistant is going to do the final steps of ENLIST: saving the patient with benefits and trial close. We call this the after diagnosis wrap-up. During these final two steps, your hygienist is going to accomplish several things.

First, she ascertains that the patient understands the diagnosis and recommended treatment. Second, that the patient understands how the treatment will guarantee the wished-for emotional value. And third, that the patient is ready to move forward. So when you exit the room, Doctor, she is going to save the patient with benefits using verbiage like in the below examples:

- "Okay, so Ms. Patient, the doctor has diagnosed a crown; a crown works much like a football helmet over your head [etc.]. Do you understand how all that works? Please feel free to ask me any questions."

Getting Clear on How to Create Value

- "What this means, Ms. Patient, is that you'll never have to worry about feeling less than confident about your smile ever again. You're not going to have to worry about the embarrassment affecting your ability to be your natural self when you try to close those real estate deals"

Then, on to the trial close. The trial close is simply asking questions to ensure that the patient understands and is ready to move forward: What questions do you have for me? What doesn't make sense? You're looking for the patient to acknowledge both the emotional value and the recommended treatment and to be ready to go.

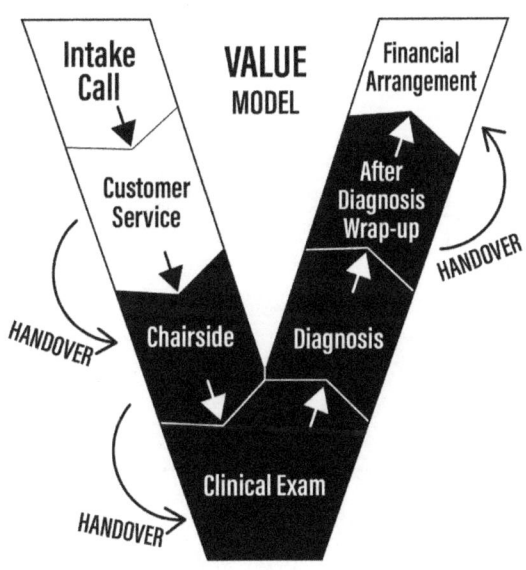

With everything covered so far, you can now see the Value Model with ENLIST broken down in each area. In the chairside step, your team member is engaging the patient, inquiring and listening to gain the emotional value and intensifying the emotional pain. She then will handover to you for the clinical exam and then diagnosis. She then will "save" the patient with benefits and trial close in the after diagnosis wrap-up.

The next chapters cover what happens before the chairside patient experience and afterward when the gathered information is handed over to the financial person.

EVERYONE GETS INVOLVED

The last chapter covered the centerpiece of where value creation takes place; however, if you're determined to have a high treatment acceptance rate, like 90–98 percent, every team member has to play a role.

Before patients show up for the initial visit, they must already have the proper mindset. The patient's mindset originates at the front desk, from the *intake* call, and culminates after the exam with the financial arrangement. When each team member knows his/her role and follows the steps in the sales process, treatment acceptance rates climb. Remember, Doctor, the continuum begins when the patient first contacts your practice.

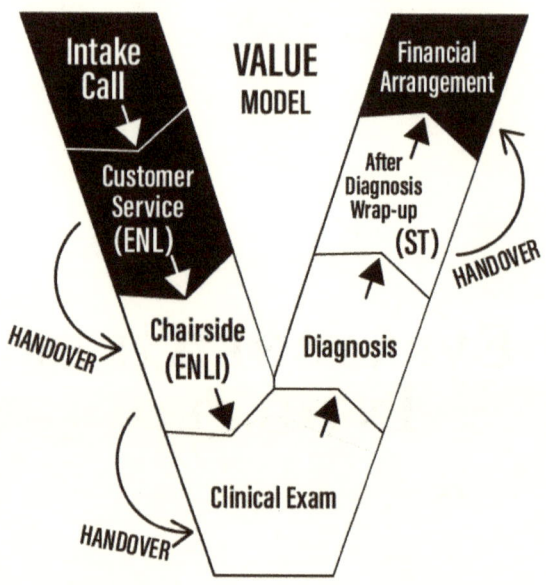

The Intake Call

The first contact a new patient has with the office is an intake call. Whether virtual or over the phone, what happens on the intake call determines the mindset that your patient brings to their appointment. With that being said, below is a perfect example of what screwing up an intake call looks like.

I travel a ridiculous number of days every year. I have one car, which I basically use to just drive to and from the airport, and it was overdue for an oil change. So, I contacted an oil change business just off the interstate between me and the airport, and I said, "Hey, I hear you guys have a special on an oil change."

"Absolutely, sir"

"Great. I will be in a hurry, so I'm going to stop by at this time. Can you make that time work?"

"Absolutely"

"Great. I'll see you then."

I'm thinking sweet, the oil change is only $19.95; I'll just show up, get the oil changed, and be on my way. However, the next day when my car is getting serviced, I'm on a phone call with a client, and after ten minutes one of the mechanics comes up to me and I can tell he needs to talk to me. I put my client on hold, and he says, "Mr. Crabtree, you need a new timing belt. You need this, you need that, you need the other thing, and you need a rear main seal." Frankly, I'm not even certain what all he said I needed. All I heard was, "It's going to be about $2,800." I said, "Wait a minute, dude, I'm on the way to catch a flight. I'm only here for a $19.95 oil change. The car drove in fine: no noise, no smoke, nothing." There's no way I was mentally prepared to drop three grand or to do anything besides the oil change.

Dental Profits

How often do patients react with surprise or outrage in your dental practice? It happens all the time. The front desk schedules the appointment, the patient shows up thinking it's going to cost them next to nothing out of pocket, but you inform the patient that they need about $12 thousand worth of dental work—no patient is prepared for that news.

In the oil change example, the situation could have gone very differently. Instead of merely scheduling the appointment for the oil change, they could have asked me some questions in the initial phone call.

> "Mr. Crabtree, before we schedule this, let me ask you, how old is your car? What's the make and model?"
>
> "It's a '98 BMW, and it has a lot of miles on it."
>
> "How many miles?"
>
> "About 155,000."
>
> "So, at what point did you change the timing belt?"
>
> "Uh . . . it's never been changed."
>
> "Oh my goodness, Mr. Crabtree. You know, the manufacturer calls for the

change at 90,000 miles, and you haven't changed it yet."

"Oh my gosh, you think that's a problem?"

"Well, I don't know. We'll take a look when you get here. When was the last time you changed your oil?"

"I really have no idea."

"Have you noticed any oil under the car where you park it?"

"Actually yeah, it's pretty bad but the oil light hasn't come on"

"Okay, that isn't supposed to happen, but again, we'll take a look when you get here."

Facilitating that exchange and asking those innocuous questions, the mechanic could have put me in a completely different mindset, and it can put your patients in a completely different mindset as well. The process for new patient intake calls is what I call LAMBS:

- **L**isten for why the patient is calling.
- **A**sk questions and take control.
- **M**agnify the answers along the way.
- **B**ring the patients to the proper realization.
- **S**et the final expectations.

The goal of the initial call isn't simply to schedule the patient but *to qualify and then schedule the patient*. You and I both know that every patient calls your practice with only one reason in mind: listen for that reason. I called the mechanic because I just needed an oil change, and that's all I was focused on; your patients call because they want to know how much you charge for a cleaning, what you charge for a root canal, how quickly they can get in, whether you take their insurance, and so on. Whatever the reason, there's only one thing that is on their mind.

How many times have you as the doctor looked in a patient's mouth and found a completely blown out situation only to have the patient say, "I'm really just here for a cleaning." When thinking about the specifics of those situations, you can see how a few questions on the intake call would have made all the difference in the world. The front desk needs to understand the LAMBS process so that they can have the patient realize that the original reason they called might not be the only reason, or even the most important reason, they should've called.

It isn't about diagnosing over the phone, it's about having the patient not be surprised at the visit. So, the front desk must *listen* to why the patient's calling, *ask* open-ended questions and take control of the conversation, *magnify* the patient's answers in an effort to *bring* the patient to the proper realization, and, finally, *set* the final expectations of the visit prior to the patient entering your dental practice.

In whatever mindset the patient leaves the call, that mindset is more than likely the same one they'll come with on the initial visit to your practice. You don't want them to enter thinking that "I just need a cleaning and it will cost nothing" only to find out that they have perio and need six crowns.

A very common call in your office goes something like this:

"Thanks for calling ABC Dental, this is Julie. I can help."

"I was wondering, do you take Delta Dental Insurance?" This is the L (listen) part of the LAMBS process and the call usually doesn't get past this first part. In most cases the question is answered, then maybe another question is answered, and Julie tries her best to schedule the patient. Most hang up without scheduling, never to be heard from again. Those who call back to schedule come in the door thinking (1) they take my insurance (2) it covers everything, and (3) I don't need any dental work, but it will be nice to get a free cleaning.

To properly qualify this patient, Julie needs to resist the urge to answer what she heard in the first step and follow through the process. Below is an example of the LAMBS process in action. See how it compares to the initial calls happening in your office currently:

>Julie: "Thanks for calling ABC Dental, this is Julie. I can help."

>Patient: "I was wondering, do you take Delta Dental Insurance?"

>Julie: "Who am I talking to?"

>Patient: "Brenda Smith."

>Julie: "Hi Brenda. Again, my name is Julie, so tell me what's going on."

Patient: "I don't really have anything going on; I just need to get a cleaning."

Julie: "When was the last time you saw a dentist?"

Patient: "It's been awhile . . . probably five years."

Julie: "What kept you away for so long?"

Patient: "I lost my insurance and now I have it back, so I just need to come in for a cleaning."

Julie: "So, let's start at the top Brenda: How often do you brush?"

Patient: "Every day."

Julie: "How many times a day?"

Patient: "Mostly once a day, usually in the morning."

Julie: "How often do you bleed when you brush?"

Patient: "Every time I brush."

Julie: "Oh, wow, that isn't supposed to happen. Have you ever been formally diagnosed with periodontal disease?"

Patient: "Yes, several years ago."

Julie: "So, you were actually diagnosed with perio . . . How long were you treated for that?"

Patient: "I never was treated for it. I went in because I lost a tooth and so I got a partial."

Julie: "Oh, you wear a partial?"

Patient: "Uh-huh."

Julie: "Okay, so what other kind of dental work have you had in the past?"

Patient: "I've had some fillings, but one of the fillings fell out."

Julie: "Did you say you lost a filling?"

Patient: "Yes. It was a white filling, and it fell out. I can tell the hole is getting larger."

Julie: "You can actually feel the hole in the tooth?"

Patient: "Yes, but it doesn't hurt yet."

Julie: "Oh my goodness! So, not yet, huh . . . we want to make sure it doesn't. What other dental work have you had?"

Patient: "I've had a several other white fillings, but I think I probably have a couple of cavities now also."

Julie: "So, you think you might have some cavities . . . What kind of sensitivity are you experiencing?"

Patient: "Anything hot or cold, or when I eat candy or something with sugar, it can hurt on the bottom, on both sides."

Julie: "Oh my, so you have a lot going on Ms. Brenda. How many chipped or broken teeth do you have?"

Patient: "I don't really have any broken or chipped, but my teeth are really brown looking, and so I don't know."

Julie: "So, you are bleeding when you brush, you've got a hole getting larger where the filling fell out, you got what feels like several cavities, and your teeth are really brown?"

Patient: "Yes, I guess I need some things done."

Julie: "Yeah, we definitely have some things to do to get you put back together. Ms. Brenda."

Patient: "I bet my insurance won't cover all that . . . Do y'all have a payment plan?"

Julie: "Absolutely. We've got all sorts of options to make it affordable—even interest free— with no money down! How's your credit?"

Patient: "Its's fine, or at least it was when I bought my car a year ago, and I haven't really bought anything big since then."

Julie: "Well, let's set you up for a new patient exam so the doctor can tell you exactly what you need. He can see you next Tuesday at 9 a.m. You'll want to plan to be here for two hours" (The final expectations are set here, followed by insurance information, personal information, and so forth.)

Julie followed the LAMBS process: *listening* to why the patient is calling, *asking* questions, and *magnifying* the patient's answers along the way, until, ultimately, Brenda is *brought* to the proper realization that she has a lot going on. Then it's a matter of *setting* the final expectations, as well as setting the appointment date and time, covering the expected length of the visit, and gathering information, which is much, much easier when the patient is in the proper mindset. No more going around and around trying to set the appointment day and time. She's ready to come in.

The above is nearly a word-for-word account of exactly how it happened in an office I've worked with for several years. It turns out Brenda needed about $6,500 worth of work; because the intake call was set up properly, she came in the door qualified. She was expecting a lot of work and ready to get it done. When the rest of the process was followed—as we'll go through next—Brenda saw value in all the dental work, and the financial arrangement made it super affordable: she prepaid and scheduled!

The Customer Service ENLIST

The next step is when the new patient shows up for his appointment. So far, the first steps in the process have been geared toward new patients, but we'll talk about existing patients in this chapter as well.

Now, when patients are properly qualified through the LAMBS process, patients not only are scheduled for an appointment but will be under the right realization, with the correct expectations. So, when the patients arrive to your office, your front desk initiates the next step in the process: *the customer service ENLIST*

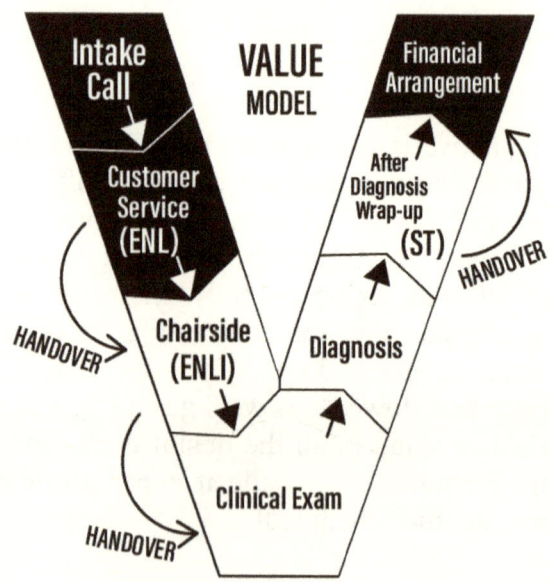

I call it the customer service ENLIST but as you can see from the value model at the beginning of this chapter, it really only includes engaging, inquiring and listening.

Just like chairside, the first step is to engage the patient: "I'm sure you noticed our vision out front, Mr. Patient. It says that we're committed to serving you at the highest level possible. If we're going to serve you at that level, then I'll need some information. It may be some questions you've never been asked before, so if you need to take a minute, please take all the time you need. So, what's most important to you about how we serve you from a customer service standpoint?"

The customer service ENLIST focuses on the first few steps: engage, inquire, and listen. This front desk process is similar to chairside value conversation, except you're trying to find out what the patient values from a customer service standpoint. So, when patients enter the office for the first visit, they're under the right realization because they've been properly qualified during the intake call. Your office is going to walk them through the new patient history and the new patient information paperwork, and then, before new patients go back to the exam room for the chairside value conversation, you're going to find out how your office can provide the best customer service experience.

After engaging the patient and the patient's response, simply inquire and listen. In the dental practices that implement this process, we have found that patients are more than eager to regale you with stories of how they were treated poorly at other practices, and exactly why they left. Patients will tell you what's important to them, and their answers will be all over the board: They made me wait, or they talked down to me. For some patients, they want the big picture, not the details; and for others, it's the opposite: they want all the details.

Your patients judge customer service in these ways. Once you have this patient information, you can note it in the patient's file and then act and react accordingly. The customer service

ENLIST not only informs you how to serve your patients at the highest level but also primes the patient for the chairside value conversation.

After the customer service ENLIST, the front desk then hands off the customer service information to the hygienist or the assistant, who begins the chairside process covered in chapter 3.

The Financial Arrangement

Remember where we are in the process. The front desk properly qualifies the patient with the intake call. The patient enters the office under the right realization. The front desk covers the customer service ENLIST and relays that information to the hygienist or the assistant, who initiates the chairside ENLIST and walks the patient through engagement, inquiring, listening, and intensifying. Then, Doctor, you come in and receive the handover. After the clinical exam, you base a diagnosis on the comprehensive examination of the heart, the mind, and the mouth, then leave. Now, the hygienist or the assistant walks through saving the patient with the benefits and trial closing. And finally, we're to the last piece of this approach: the handover to the financial arrangement. Believe it or not, this is the easiest part of the whole process.

I know, while you're reading this, you're probably thinking, Man, that is not the case in my practice: it sometimes takes forty-five minutes to wrap up the financials. That's because none of the above process takes place in your practice, and so your financial conversation isn't really about finances, it's about the treatment.

The first step is to properly assign the person who will handle the financial arrangement with the patient. If this person has been previously titled the treatment coordinator, or as the person presenting the treatment, change that. He or she should be the financial coordinator, or some title that explains the role. The treatment should be coordinated *before* talking about finances; treatment and finances are two very different things. Remember, with everything that has been done in this process, the treatment has been *presented* by the doctor and thoroughly explained by the hygienist or the assistant. We're now ready for the financial arrangement.

When the patient understands the treatment, the financial coordinator doesn't need to walk the patient through the treatment plan; as a matter-of-fact, doing so will further complicate the issue. Because of ENLIST, patients understand that the treatment will fulfill their emotional value, so they're ready for the financial aspect of the treatment.

Now, the financial conversation should be nothing more than the financials. Your financial coordinator is going to love this. He or she has struggled for too long with trying to talk about the money, only to have the patient ask clinical questions. Also, since none of the treatment understanding has been in place, your financial coordinator has to begin the financial conversation by walking the patient through the treatment, which invites questions and muddies the waters. Under the methodology detailed in this book, the financial conversation is the easiest step in the entire process.

The financial process follows the acronym RPM:

- **R**eceive the handover.
- **P**lace the responsibility squarely on the patient's shoulders.
- **M**ake it as easy as possible for the patient to say yes.

The financial coordinator receives the handover from the hygienist or the assistant, places the financial responsibility squarely on the patients shoulders, and makes it as easy as possible for the patient to say yes. No longer is the financial coordinator also the treatment coordinator.

The handover from the hygienist or assistant to the financial coordinator is based directly on the after diagnosis wrap-up (chapter 3) and should communicate the following four items: (1) the patient understands the treatment and has no questions, (2) the patient understands how the treatment will satisfy the their emotional value, (3) the intensification piece (how its affected the patient now and in the past), and (4) that the patient is ready to go.

How might that handover go? The hygienist or assistant isn't going to bring up the clinical stuff. That's gone over and done. The handover makes it as easy as possible for the financial coordinator to close the deal.

Here's how a handover might run (Julie is the financial coordinator):

"Julie, you remember Sean; Sean and I have had a great conversation. The most important thing to Sean is that he wants the confidence that can only come from a nice, white, straight smile. He's dealt with insecurity over his smile since he was eighteen years old. It's affecting not only his confidence but his ability to make real estate sales because he's always covering his mouth and not able to be his normal outgoing self. The doctor has diagnosed a comprehensive treatment plan. I know you have that plan Julie, and Sean and I have walked through the whole treatment. He understands how it all works, and most importantly, he understands that once the treatment is complete, he'll never have to worry about feeling insecure or less than confident ever again. Julie, he's ready to go."

Right now, the handover to financials in your office is full of dental jargon, such as tooth numbers, mesial, buccal, occlusal, and the like . . . it's all Greek and, therefore, has no place in the handover. Your patients tune it out; they're not paying attention. As a result, any value that may have been created is lost. The financial coordinator, Julie, should receive the handover and turn to the patient and say to the hygienist, "Thanks Beckie. Okay, Sean, looks like we can do that for zero down, zero interest, and $399 a month." Always present in monthly terms.

Why present in monthly terms? Two very good reasons: (1) to make it as easy as possible for patients to say yes and (2) to support your schedule, your team, and your bottom line.

Let's start with the first reason. There are many articles written on the statistics of consumer preference to monthly payments. A recent article on Business Wire (2018) reports a survey that found that "62% of consumers would prefer fixed monthly plans with clear payment terms"; also, the article says that "76% of U.S. consumers are more likely to make a retail purchase if a payment plan backed by a simple and seamless point of sale experience is offered."

You want to be on an equal playing field with your competitors, and your competitors aren't dentists. They are companies competing for the same discretionary dollars as you, and they make it easy by offering monthly plans.

Your competitors are, for example, Ford Motor Credit, Honda Motor Credit, Disney Cruise Line, Southwest Airlines, Home Depot, Best Buy, and the list goes on. Every one of these companies offers monthly terms because they understand that their sales (treatment acceptance) will be 50–80 percent higher when they make it as easy as possible to say yes—for example, Best Buy promotes the sales of its 84-inch flatscreen TVs with monthly installments and zero down: just sign your name here and leave with your purchase. If your patient can sign their name for a flatscreen, why would you want to make buying your dentistry more difficult by asking for the $500 all at once.

Reason two: monthly terms support your schedule, your team, and your profitability. As I write this, I'm looking at numbers from a practice that I recently had this conversation with. When I first started working with them, the collection rate was 85 percent of adjusted production. To be clear, that means that for every dollar they produced, one dollar was adjusted (for insurance) to, say, around seventy cents, and then they collected 85 percent of the seventy cents. Here is another way to say that: for every real dollar they produced, they collected sixty cents; a real collection rate of 60 percent. After getting this concept, this team has really been utilizing the processes and presenting everything in monthly terms. Utilizing third-party financing and presenting in monthly terms allows that some portion of what they collect is ahead of production. In other words, the practice receives payment before the case is actually produced. As of now, their real collection rate is 102 percent, which means that for every real dollar (not adjusted) that they produce they collect a dollar and two cents! Just like Southwest Airlines, Amazon, Disney Cruise Lines, Sandals Resorts, and so on, the list goes on and on.

So, maximizing third-party and presenting in monthly terms are obviously good for the bottom line, but the higher value is in your schedule. Cancels and no-shows are drastically reduced because procedures in the schedule have been, in some portion, previously collected. Monthly terms also support the team, because absent a real emergency, what's in the schedule can be counted on, and the front doesn't have to stop what they're doing and spend endless amounts of energy on filling holes the same day.

So, your financial coordinator receives the handover, presents the monthly financial terms and parks it squarely with the patient, and makes it as easy as possible for the patient to say yes (RPM). After Jenny, (your hygienist) hands over the patient (Sean) to your financial coordinator (Julie), a real example could sound something like this:

Julie: "Thanks Jenny. Okay, Sean, looks like we can do that for $268 per month."

Sean: "Okay, how much does my insurance cover?"

Julie: "That's everything after your insurance. That's $268 per month, nothing down and interest free!"

Sean: "So I don't pay you anything today?"

Julie: "No, it's no money down and just $268 per month. I'll get the paperwork going now."

Sean: "How much am I paying total out of pocket?"

Julie: "That would be $268 per month for 24 months. Is there a better monthly payment that works for you?"

Sean: "No, I can do that."

Julie: "Give me just a second and I'll get it started."

Lastly, the financial coordinator helps the patient complete the application and closes the case and schedules the next visit. At this point, she then can walk the patient through the details of exactly what to expect in terms of how the third party works: when to expect the first bill, how the interest or interest-free works, and in general just making sure the patient fully understands and has no questions. It really is that easy.

DEFINE THE ROLES, FOCUS ON OUTCOMES, AND EXCITE YOUR TEAM

Let's recap the Value Model steps:

1. **Intake Call:** The front desk qualifies the patient using the LAMBS process.
2. **The Customer Service ENLIST:** When the patient arrives for the appointment, the front desk walks the patient through the customer service ENLIST—engagement and inquiring and listening—walks the new patient through the paperwork, and prepares the patient for the chairside exam.

The front desk hands overs to the hygienist or the assistant.

3. **Chairside ENLIST:** The hygienist or the assistant starts the chairside comprehensive exam by engaging the patient and the next three steps of ENLIST, and hands over their findings to the doctor.

4. **Diagnosis:** The doctor performs the clinical exam, makes a diagnosis, and moves on.

5. **The After Diagnosis Wrap-up:** The hygienist or the assistant completes the final two steps of ENLIST and hands over the patient to the financial coordinator.

6. **Financial Arrangement:** The financial coordinator goes through RPM with the patient.

Clearly Defining Roles

In an ideal world, the same front-desk person who handles the intake call is the same one who walks the patient through the customer service ENLIST and who ends the patient's visit with the financial arrangement. If you have five people at the front desk, then two of them should be doing nothing but intake calls, customer service ENLISTs, and financial arrangements. In this way, the same people working the front desk who have developed a relationship with the patient— beginning during the intake call—are there for the patient from the beginning to the end of every visit, reinforcing that relationship.

The intake call is the only big difference between new patients and existing patients. In subsequent visits, existing patients are already accustomed to your office, having been properly qualified and placed in the right mindset with the right expectation on their first visit. So, essentially, you are picking up with existing patients chairside, where the hygienist or the assistant will go through the ENLIST.

When beginning to implement this methodology, you can walk existing patients through the customer service ENLIST; in fact, many of the offices I work with do that. They just have the existing patient show up a little early to their visit and will also use this time to update health history and any new policies. Many offices want to ensure every existing patient keeps the right mindset and the right expectations; they see value in reminding existing patients about their commitment to serve and in inquiring of patients to find out how they can best be served.

The steps talked about in this book are a part of an overall strategy we call the *Sincerity Approach*. Many dental offices have steps to follow in all aspects of the business, from clinical processes to answering the phone, but the key difference between our approach and others is that our approach isn't task based. Ultimately, you can't be successful if your team is focused on the performance of tasks: they have to be clear about the outcome they're trying to achieve. And how exactly what they do from minute to minute is connected to it. They should be thinking at all times what it is that they are *sincerely* trying to accomplish rather than what they're supposed to *do*. Outcomes as opposed to tasks. Doctor, it's key that you talk with all your team about their individual roles until they each understand sincerely what it is that each is trying to achieve. I've learned, over the last twenty-two years, that in dentistry, people frame everything in tactical steps. There's nothing necessarily wrong with that as long as the purpose, *the sincere outcome* of those steps is kept in focus.

Let's take the intake call as an example. You don't want the front desk person to simply follow the steps, you want them to sincerely focus on whether or not the patient is properly qualified. So, in the intake call, the person handling the call must understand the number one priority in the LAMBS process: to properly qualify the patient. And what is properly qualifying the patient? When the patient realizes that the initial reason for the call (e.g., When can I be seen for a cleaning?) isn't the reason on which the patient should be focused; for example, the patient should be focused on possible periodontal disease or a missing tooth that needs care. And it's up to the front desk to follow the steps of the intake call—the LAMBS process—to refocus the patient from the initial reason for the call. Ultimately, the role of the intake-call person is to ensure that the patient arrives at the office under the right realization, with the right expectation. No one, you or the patient, wants to get any surprises.

For the chairside component, Doctor, make sure that your hygienist or your assistant knows their role in engaging the patient, ensuring that patients understand how answering the following questions will benefit them and making patients comfortable enough to share their heart so that their emotional value can be discovered. And make sure their focus is not on doing the engagement but instead on sincerely accomplishing these two things.

Doctor, after you've given your diagnosis and left, your hygienist or your assistant must focus on sincerely ensuring that the patient understands the treatment and how the treatment will get his or her desired emotional value. After answering all the patient's questions, the hygienist or assistant hands over the patient to the financial coordinator.

The role of the financial coordinator is actually very simple. The financial coordinator's role is not simply to follow the RPM steps but to sincerely focus on receiving the handover, parking the financial squarely on the patient's shoulders, and making it as easy as possible for the patient to say yes.

In the next chapter, I go into the nitty-gritty challenges of each of these roles and how to track whether each role is getting the right outcome. But for now, let's go over how to think about outcomes with your team.

Think about Outcomes with Your Team

Your team must not only clearly understand their individual roles but also not view themselves as employees—the success of this whole process depends on it. Their perspective starts with you, Doctor: you can't think of your team as people who perform tasks, think of your team as people who create outcomes. Everything in this book is outcomes-based and everything in your practice should be as well. When the front desk person conducts an intake call and goes through each step of the LAMBS process, then, by all accounts, all the tasks were performed—but it doesn't matter if the right outcome isn't achieved.

You want to create a culture where your team views themselves as partners in your business. Aside from their individual roles, each team member must understand the team's overall objective, the overall outcome that they're trying to achieve. Doctor, you must communicate with your team daily to make sure that each team member is connecting what they're trying to achieve with the overall outcomes the team is trying to achieve. Your team must be clear on their individual roles and understand how not only the specific role but the roles of the other members work together to meet the team's objective. So, Doctor, you must put what you're trying to achieve out in front of everything by prioritizing and communicating the outcome.

Get your team to understand and believe that a patient leaving with clean teeth but not accepting the treatment that they need isn't serving the patient at the highest level. You want to communicate to your team, constantly repeating that patients who accept comprehensive dentistry are served at a higher level. Consequently, for us on this team, if more patients accept treatment, more dentistry gets done, and the office doesn't need to take on as many patients. With fewer patients and more treatment acceptance, the team can provide a higher level of care to patients. No more crown-of-the-month club, no more herds of patients, and no more running from patient to patient to do single units of work. It's good for the patients, good for the team, and good for the bottom line.

I'm talking about creating a completely different dentistry environment. Your team must connect what they're trying to accomplish in their individual roles to the team's overall objective. Doctor, your office can do a higher amount of dentistry on fewer patients when the following are its objective:

- higher collections
- higher rate of collections
- comprehensive diagnoses
- comprehensive treatments

Maybe fewer patients aren't your goal. Nonetheless, every doctor who reads this book endeavors to serve their patients at the highest level of care possible. And so, when patients accept the dentistry they want and need, when patients accept comprehensive treatment, *you will be serving them at a higher level*.

You've got to prioritize and communicate every day to your team the following: how the individual objectives of each role connect and contribute to the overall outcome.

In the next section, we're going to go over the bonus system. While money alone will not be enough to keep great people accomplishing great things, a properly designed bonus can help direct your team's focus and be a big part of motivation.

Team Bonuses

Many of you come to this part of the chapter from a lot of different angles. Some of you are thinking, "Oh no, not another bonus. I've tried it in the past, but bonuses don't work. I had to pull them, which was horrible." Whereas, some of you haven't done bonuses and are curious about how they might work. After working with dentists and dental teams for twenty-two years all over North America, I've come across a lot of really goofy bonus systems, most of which don't work.

Bonuses should be a carrot that when achieved, the business has achieved a greater level of financial success and, therefore, is able to absorb paying the bonus. Most bonus systems are not rooted in this way, so they don't accomplish what they set out to achieve. And when a bonus system doesn't work, and doctors end up pulling bonuses, it kills any and all motivation in your staff. So, if you're going to introduce a bonus system, make sure the bonus system is rooted in the proper financial outcome. For instance, a bonus system according to production isn't rooted in the proper outcome. You could end up like one client I had who, when we first met, was paying a bonus determined by increases over a certain number in production, and because of that, he ended up paying out monies that weren't collected on. An American Dental Association (ADA) (2019) stat shows that over a ten-year period, from 2007 through 2017, dentists in the US were producing more but earning the same—in my experience less—so if you have a bonus system rooted in production, you are rewarding the wrong thing.

The goal isn't to produce more but to increase profits. Doctor, you want a bonus system rooted in profitability. A bonus will be proper only when it rewards according to proper outcomes.

Having begun to institute an outcome-based practice, you want to reward people who are thinking beyond the performance of tactical tasks, right? You don't want your team to perform the ENLIST, LAMBS, or RPM process and think, "I'm just an employee, I did my job. I did what was asked." A bonus system must elicit a sincerity-based mindset in your team.

Your bonus system should be designed to unburden your team members from the employee mindset and help them think like partners in your business. You're not looking for them to perform tasks or do steps—you're looking for your people to sincerely own the outcomes in their particular role and connect the outcomes with the overall purpose of the team and dental practice.

The bonus should be monthly and easy to calculate. So easy that the team can create goals every single month according to the number of dollars they want in bonus. Again, as long as this bonus is rooted in profitability, Doctor, you'll want to pay as big a bonus as possible!

To create a proper bonus, you'll want to set a baseline for your type of practice. There's an easy formula, according to the type of practice you have, to create your baseline (and if you contact me, I'm happy to share it). For the sake of brevity and the purposes of this book, calculate your overhead, add a cushion for the unexpected, and then set this number as a baseline. That number should include all the bills, payroll taxes, insurance, loan repayment, and the like. Include every ounce of expenses you have, except your pay, then add extra. The team would then get a bonus as a percentage of the overage collected above that baseline number.

As for what percentage they should get for a bonus, it depends on the benchmark percentage of payroll. If yours is a general practice, then the benchmark percentage for payroll in your practice should be 20 percent of net income. In other words, for your practice to be financially healthy, no more than 20 percent of your net income should go out in payroll. That means the team will split 20 percent of this overage in collections beyond the baseline amount.

The bonus should be paid monthly but according to the average of the last three months. In other words, if average collections for November, December, and January are over the baseline amount, then a bonus will be achieved and paid for in January. And so, a February bonus depends on December, January, and February average collections and the like. Having a bonus rooted in a three-month average smooths out the peaks that are natural in business and protects you from paying out a single month bonus on a fluke month.

WHAT TO TRACK, WHEN TO TRACK, AND HOW TO USE THE INFORMATION

In the last chapter, we talked about defining roles and giving bonuses. Now, we'll talk about how to track the outcomes of your team to inform how you give bonuses and how to use the information from tracking to conduct meaningful team meetings in your practice.

Commitment to Tracking

If you haven't figured it out by now, Doctor, everything we've talked about requires a different commitment from you. It's a commitment to your business on a daily scenario. You can't expect massive results if your focus is 100 percent on the clinical aspects of your practice. Way too often I see doctors invest money into a new procedure, thinking that "if I could just do implants, sleep, Botox, vampire facelifts (yep), and the like, my practice will take off." Doctor, stop wasting money on learning new clinical procedures. None of these will grow your business if you cannot create value for the procedures you're currently offering. This profession is full of very talented, overeducated clinical standouts who cannot make a decent living. And you can't half-heartedly invest your time and your focus on your business and expect massive results. What you and your team prioritize in your practice must completely change.

You need to make treatment acceptance a big focus overall, and that starts with everyone getting on the same page. Each team member is trying to accomplish something: you want them to clearly see how their specific role contributes to the practice's overall purpose, whether the goal is to have fewer patients with higher production and collections, to work fewer days with greater results, or even to cut the hours per day while still increasing results. Whatever the goal, to get there, treatment acceptance is the key.

So, what are you tracking? You should be tracking the dollars of treatment that were presented versus the dollars of treatment that were paid —for every single patient, every single day. It's like baseball: you're tracking how many times you stand at the plate versus how many times you get on base. And further, how you got on base: Was it a walk? a single? a double? a triple? a homerun? Also, you want to track the strikeouts: to get that information, you have to track every single presentation, every single day.

You're probably thinking, "What if I presented treatment that wasn't accepted by the patient, then the patient goes back into the hygiene program, but then I re-present treatment another time? Do I count that?" Yes, because that's another at bat—you're trying to track the at bats: how many times you stand at the plate versus how many times you get on base.

You're tracking every single presentation, every single day, no matter what. Tracking this way is clean, simple, and the best way for you to measure how well you're doing at creating value.

Accepted Is Paid For

Over two decades ago, when I entered the dental world, I was surprised to learn that offices weren't tracking treatment acceptance; it's the most important data and yet dental offices rarely if ever tracked it. Of the less than 1 percent of dentists I ran into who tracked treatment acceptance, they were tracking it completely wrong, counting scheduled treatment as accepted, whether paid for or not.

I worked with Dr. Murphy for about four years before his retirement. When I first met the doctor, he was so excited to tell me that his office had an 86 percent treatment acceptance rate and yet he couldn't understand how his profitability was so low; he wasn't able to pay himself several months out of the year. My offices shoot for a 98 percent acceptance rate, so I knew something wasn't right. Well, in watching his office work for a day, I knew that 86 percent wasn't close to right. When I began diving into what was working and what wasn't, I began with the statistics and discovered that, among other things, he was tracking treatment acceptance as scheduled, not as paid for.

For instance, a common scenario might be for a patient to arrive at the front desk after an exam with $6,500 of work needed, the first step of which is an SRP (scaling and root planning). If the patient scheduled the SRP, the whole case was counted as accepted. You probably know where I'm going with this example: the patient wouldn't show up for the appointment and hadn't paid anything up front, but Dr. Murphy's office tracked the case as accepted. There was no financial commitment, and Dr. Murphy wasn't tracking that anywhere. To add insult to injury, he had created what he called a bonus for his front desk. In some cases, he was paying her a percentage of the total amount "accepted"! She would get a percentage of $6,500 that the practice never collected a penny on—that can definitely affect your ability to pay yourself!

Dr. Murphy was excited by the thought of an 86 percent acceptance rate, but when we started counting accepted only as paid for, we discovered that he fell into the same category as most dental practices who aren't implementing these strategies. The 86 percent treatment acceptance was actually only about 19 percent.

The moral of the story is to track what's accepted only as what's paid for. To be specific, Doctor, you want to track what treatment is presented to the patient versus what treatment is paid for. So, if a patient is presented with $6,500 worth of work, track that. If you're taking insurance, of course, take that out of the mix. The patient pays all their copay and fees, so insurance and the write off (if PPO) covers the balance: we'll call that 100 percent accepted. If no insurance, collect the whole balance but make it easy, as in monthly terms.

To break this transaction down further, ask: How much was presented? Did the patient schedule? How much, if any, is expected in insurance? How much was paid? What was the collection opportunity? Below are two examples of when $6,500 is presented to the patient:

Patient	Amount ($)	Scheduled	Insurance ($)	Paid ($)	Collection Opportunity ($)
John Smith	6,500	Yes	No	6,500	6,500
Jack Johnson	6,500	Yes	1,200	500	5,300

In the above table, we see John Smith is exactly what we're shooting for: 100 percent accepted. Jack Johnson, on the other hand, leaves opportunity. His treatment is $6,500, and insurance is estimated at $1,200; therefore, we have a $5,300 opportunity to collect and have only collected $500. Either Jack Johnson didn't accept all the treatment or he didn't pay for everything he scheduled. There's a solution we can apply here: the solution can be found between the intake call and the financial.

Doctor, this method of tracking is meaningful because it serves your practice and your patients. If a scheduled patient doesn't in fact pay, then, as you already know, the money can stand between them and whether they actually show up for the next appointment; that is, they only scheduled, they didn't accept; only if treatment is paid for can it truly be accepted.

Tracking in this way can also push you to think about how you're presenting the finances, which holds accountability and informs potential practice improvements; if third party financing isn't being utilized and cash is being asked for instead, that can be why the whole case wasn't accepted. Remember the example given earlier about a flat screen TV? You want to be as easy to do business with as buying that flatscreen TV. The easier it is, the more treatment is accepted. Tracking in this way can allow for those inefficiencies to show up early and often, so you make sure you're utilizing third-party financing at the highest level.

How to Have Meetings

Hopefully, at this point, with everything we've talked about so far in this book, you can now get excited about meetings. It should be apparent that meetings are when this communication and tracking and coaching all takes place. While morning meetings are common in most dental practices, their purpose is usually only to go over the schedule for the day. While there may be things that should be talked about regarding the schedule, most of what is discussed can be determined by simply looking at it. I'm not talking about that kind of meeting. I'm talking about meetings geared differently so that the focus is on the success of the business for that day.

Morning meetings should happen every single day and include the schedule and other small details. They should have a specific focus in mind: prepare your team for where your presentations might happen on that day, who will do what, and who needs what, so that every opportunity can be closed. Any requests about preparedness that need to be made while the whole team is together can happen in morning meetings.

In morning meetings, new patient financials or existing patient's financials, or any combination that might result in patients being released at the same time, should be reviewed and specific requests made. Also, for example, for an existing patient coming in that day with previously diagnosed work, assign who will ENLIST, and specifically clarify the solution the hygienist or the assistant will implement, because value wasn't created last time with that patient. The financial coordinator, the hygienists, the assistants should all make whatever requests necessary so that everyone knows who's doing what and what the expectations are for the day. Walking into the day without these plans in place is planning to fail.

Afternoon meetings—I'm shocked at the number of dentists who don't have afternoon meetings—have a very meaningful place in the daily operations of your practice, especially now that you've put the proper tracking in place and specifically because each day begins with plans being made. The afternoon meeting covers what worked and what didn't for that day. This is your problem-solving time and it can't happen in any other part of the day. Remember, you're tracking every presentation, every single patient, every single day. The meeting is about all the specifics: Sean Crabtree was in today; we presented $12,000 worth of work; he accepted only $1,000 of it. You want to go over possible reasons why Sean didn't accept all the presented treatment. Was Sean a new patient? If so, did we have him properly qualified on the intake call? What specifically happened on that call? Where's the opportunity? If it wasn't on the intake call, what happened during the customer service ENLIST? What about the chairside ENLIST? Doctor, what did you get as an emotional value handed over to you? Financial Coordinator, what did you get handed over to you? Note of caution: if Sean Crabtree didn't schedule the treatment, the solution lies somewhere in this process, between the intake call and the financial arrangement. Do what's necessary to keep the conversation about which ball was dropped and what we'll do to prevent it tomorrow. Spending even a single minute on some story about how Sean was concerned about insurance coverage or a bad experience his first cousin's husband's sister had here last year . . . all a complete waste of time and simply a way to kill the ability to get to the solutions.

Every day, your office dives into the specific cases of the day to find a solution, a solution everyone can learn and implement tomorrow. You should always be striving to improve tomorrow and the day after tomorrow, so that in three-weeks' time you're in a completely different place.

In addition to morning and afternoon meetings, I would challenge you to set up a weekly meeting, always at the same time, on the same day, every single week. These weekly meetings will accomplish the big picture items. A weekly meeting should be an hour to an hour and a half, depending on the size of your practice. If you're a $600,000 a month practice with a nineteen-person team, meetings need to go an hour and a half; if you're a normal bread-and-butter practice, doing $2.9 million a year with seven to nine team members, then an hour meeting is probably sufficient.

In the weekly meeting, address broader questions about what's working and what's not: What trends are we seeing on qualifying patients from the intake call? If we are consistently getting patients who don't schedule and need to talk to their spouse, we need training on those specifics. Who will set it up and when? What should we do differently on the handover to the doctor? If we're getting great emotional values but they're not getting to the doctor in front of the patient, we need to change our process for how and when that happens before the exam. Who will create that plan and when? What's trending on financial arrangements? If we have a 90 percent treatment acceptance rate but the financials are taking forty minutes, the financial coordinator is either doing too many things or not getting handovers in front of the patient. Who is creating a plan for the change and when?

The morning and afternoon meetings are in the details. In the morning, address the following: Who's coming in with opportunities? Who on the team is going to do what? How are we going to approach it? And in the afternoon, ask, What happened? Like other professional companies, focus on the process - the intake call LAMBS, the chairside ENLIST, financial conversations and the handovers - each step in the process. For example if you're having an issue with the financial conversation, role play in the afternoon meeting to learn what could be done differently. If this goes long, make it a training for the weekly meeting. Your team is going to make mistakes in every one of those steps...it's expected and all part of the learning process.

Coach It Consistently and Reap the Rewards

Your team must focus on not only the performance of their job but the overall strategy of what they're trying to accomplish. This type of long-term thinking is echoed in Michael Gerber's (2004) book *E-Myth: Why Most Small Businesses Don't Work and What to Do About It*. Gerber talks about the technical versus the strategic. In summary, America is the greatest country on earth; only in America can anyone become what they want. If you enjoy making great pizza, you can open a pizza restaurant; if you enjoy dentistry, you can become a dentist and open a practice. However, Gerber is making a broader point here: if you want to start a small business simply because you're passionate about/good at/ enjoy something, then you don't have the right mindset, you're focusing only on the tactical aspects and not on what it takes to have that become a successful business

According to the Small Business Administration, only about a third of small businesses in the US ever make it past the ten-year mark. The reason is Gerber's point exactly. The person who opened the pizza restaurant really enjoys making great pizza, but making great pizza doesn't directly translate to running a successful pizza business—in reality, it has little to do with success.

There's a lot you can learn from this, Doctor. Being a great dentist and performing competent clinical skills has no bearing whatsoever on whether you can build, or have built, a very successful dental business. What separates a single doctor with $680,000 general practice and a single doctor with a $3 million general practice has nothing to do with clinical skills, demographics, area, or type and locations of building. Doctor, as the captain of the ship, where you focus determines the trajectory of your business.

To reap the rewards of your business, you must shift your focus. I realize this can be difficult in dentistry, especially because dentistry can be viewed as a technical process. But you must shift your focus from only being great at clinical dentistry to prioritizing being great at your dental business. Or in Gerber's words: shift your focus from working *in* your business to working *on* your business!

Business success requires you and your team to consistently apply, maintain, and sustain the right strategic thinking. You don't want to zero in on the tasks your team is performing, such as flipping rooms, seeing patients, and scheduling patients. As captain of the ship, you must constantly be focused on the big picture, because the minute it veers, the process and progress quickly go away. As the doctor, you must prioritize and coach a consistent strategy—that's your role.

Giving It to You Straight

In 2017, for my podcast Dental Profits, I interviewed Matt Manero, a multimillion-dollar business owner in Texas and author of *You Need More Money*. I began the interview by quoting some statistics aloud in a lead up to my questions. I said to Matt how I was surprised to learn that in the US only a little above 5 percent of small businesses ever gross more than a million dollars and that 99 percent of the businesses in the US are small businesses. He interrupted me right away, saying that it was too much. I asked what he meant. He told me what I had witnessed every day for the last twenty plus years: that being a small business owner in the US is tough and that there are way too many people out there who are pretending to be business owners; they enjoy doing the do, but don't enjoy what it takes to have a successful business, and so it doesn't happen. They're suffering, their businesses are suffering, and their employees are suffering—they're just not successful at all.

I have worked with struggling businesses and suffering teams over and over and over again in dentistry. Like it or not, Doctor, you're captain of this ship, and the success of the business is 100 percent on you. Everything you decide, where your attention is, what questions you ask, all determine the success of your business.

If you want to *only* focus on performing high-quality clinical dentistry, there's nothing wrong with that, but you don't need to own a business (again, there's nothing wrong with that). Be in education; academia is great, or work for somebody who's willing to shoulder the responsibility of being captain of the ship. However, Doctor, you're teasing yourself if you only focus on doing the clinical work and expect a successful business: you're going to be upset when your business struggles—right now is your wake-up call.

As the captain, Doctor, your team pays attention to what you ask about; and as a result, what you pay attention to gets done. If you don't pay attention to the things that promote business success—such as the steps in the sales process outlined in this book—then you can't expect success. Not asking the right questions; not setting clear expectations for your team, yourself, and your business; and not doing this daily, weekly, monthly, and yearly will only ensure that the proper process dissipates and disappears.

The Mick Jagger effect doesn't apply to your dental business. You cannot put all your focus on being a great singer and at the same time expect that a hundred thousand people will flock to the arena and anxiously await your arrival—to simply show up and sing. When you only focus on being a great clinician, you'll have great clinical outcomes; however, you won't have a successful dental business. I'm not suggesting that you remove focus from being a great clinician, but you need to give equal—if not more—focus to having a successful dental business. Shift your focus: monitor and give active attention to the processes that serve your business and utilize meetings around what these processes are designed to do. I know having a great clinical outcome comes natural to you: you're a great clinician. But, if during meetings, for example, your focus centers only on minutia, like flipping rooms or instrument handoffs, you won't have a successful dental business.

If your practice is suffering, don't put pressure on yourself: ease off the gas. Remove the mindset that doing more on top of more of the same will result in business success—rethink your whole approach so that it meshes with everything covered in this book.

WTF

Doctor, you're the captain and the coach. You must give attention to the right things, ask the right questions, and give properly informed and consistent direction. Your focus and questioning should be centered around what your team is thinking. Remember from chapter one: be, do, have. How you're *be*ing in your mind will determine the things that you'll *do* and what you do determines what you get to *have* (the results that you're after).

The same is true for the people on your team. Every day that you're in a morning, afternoon, or weekly meeting, and you look at your team, ask yourself WTF? Where's the focus? First, find your focus, because it determines what you ask them and how you ask it. Second, find their focus. When you hear the answers your team gives, it's a window into their focus and how they are thinking. Be, first. Do, second. Have, third. For your business to be successful there is nothing in the dental office that is *only* do, and as the captain, you're the standard bearer of this concept.

Tough-No

If you have made it this far into this book, you're probably thinking one of two ways: Either you are a little overwhelmed and seriously questioning whether or not you want to continue in this entrepreneurial journey or you see the possibilities and are excited to begin implementation. My aim is that it's the latter.

As I write this final chapter, I just got off a team meeting with a current client in the Midwest; we'll call him Dr. Jason. In the past Jason and his team were working just like I previously worked—*hard*. They had added Saturdays and two longer days during the week to the schedule. He wanted badly to have more time with his family and specifically to help coach his son's football team, but he didn't see it as possible. Since we began working together, Dr. Jason has focused relentlessly on the implementation of the sincerity methodology and, specifically, on coaching his team on the sales strategies covered in these pages. He has become the person who enjoys putting focus on the business aspects of dentistry, and it's paying off big time. In the last three months he and his team have worked nearly two weeks less and collected nearly $300,000 more than the same three-month period last year.

His team is excited to collect a bonus this month of $1,130 per person. You and your team can too.

While I have witnessed firsthand many dentists who struggle in their business—and I wholeheartedly agree with Matt Manero that most enjoy doing the *do* and not what it takes to have a successful dental business—I do not agree that it's tough. It is simply a matter of taking the first two chapters in this book to heart and learning to enjoy the business aspects that allow you to perform more of the *do* that you already enjoy. If you become the person who enjoys implementation of the strategies covered, you can grow your dental business without spending your career on the constant chase for endless amounts of new patients. If you switch your focus from only clinical greatness to business greatness, you can grow without adding days and hours to your schedule. Hard work does not equal success—working on the right things equals success, and it isn't necessary to be shot in the head to gain that perspective. You can do this. If not for your own health and sanity, then do it because, as I've learned, there is no greater feeling in the world than making shifts in yourself that allow you to make a difference in the lives of the people you serve, your team, and your family.

I'm convinced that successful entrepreneurship is at the very heart of the American dream and that being allowed to be at the helm of your own destiny is in many ways uniquely and inherently American. A mentor of mine was known to say, "You only get one shot at this life and mama ain't coming, it's up to you to make it the best it can be". My sincerest hope is that this book becomes part of what drives you to seek the very best from yourself and to pursue success at the highest level for your business!

For more information, please visit

www.thecrabtreegroup.com

REFERENCES

American Dental Association. 2019. "Dental Practice." Health Policy Institute. https://www.ada.org/en/science-research/health-policy-institute/data-center/dental-practice

Bechara, Antoine. 2004. "The Role of Emotion in Decision-Making: Evidence from Neurological Patients with Orbitofrontal Damage." *Brain and Cognition* 55 (1): 30–40. http://doi: 10.1016/j.bandc.2003.04.001.

Business Insider. 2018. "76% Of Consumers Are More Likely to Make a Purchase If a Simple and Seamless Payment Plan is Offered." Business Insider.

https://www.businesswire.com/news/home/20181108005056/en/76-Consumers-Purchase-Simple-Seamless-Payment-Plan.

Carson, Ben. 2010. "Ben Carson: An Extraordinary Life - Conversations from Penn State." Interview posted on May 7, 2010. YouTube. https://www.youtube.com/watch?v=4-8NRSfk_a8&ab_channel=wpsu. Please note that this is not the exact interview mentioned in the text but covers the same material.

Gerber, Michael E. 2004. *E-Myth: Why Most Small Businesses Don't Work and What to Do About It*. New York: Harper Business.

www.ingramcontent.com/pod-product-compliance
Lightning Source LLC
Chambersburg PA
CBHW022114090426
42743CB00008B/848

9781948382076